UKULELE Peace, Hope & Love

ISBN 978-1-4803-3994-1

HAL•LEONARD® CORPORATION

7777 W. BLUEMOUND RD. P.O. BOX 13819 MILWAUKEE, WI 53213

Visit Hal Leonard Online at
www.halleonard.com

All You Need Is Love

Words and Music by John Lennon and Paul McCartney

First note

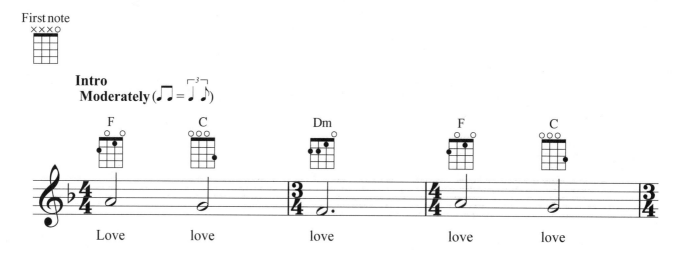

Intro
Moderately

Love   love   love   love   love

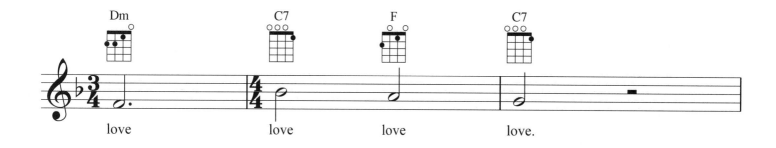

love   love   love   love.

(*Instrumental*)

Verse

1. There's noth-ing you can do   that   can't be   done. _____
2. There's noth-ing you can make   that   can't be   made. _____
3. There's noth-ing you can know   that   is-n't   known. _____

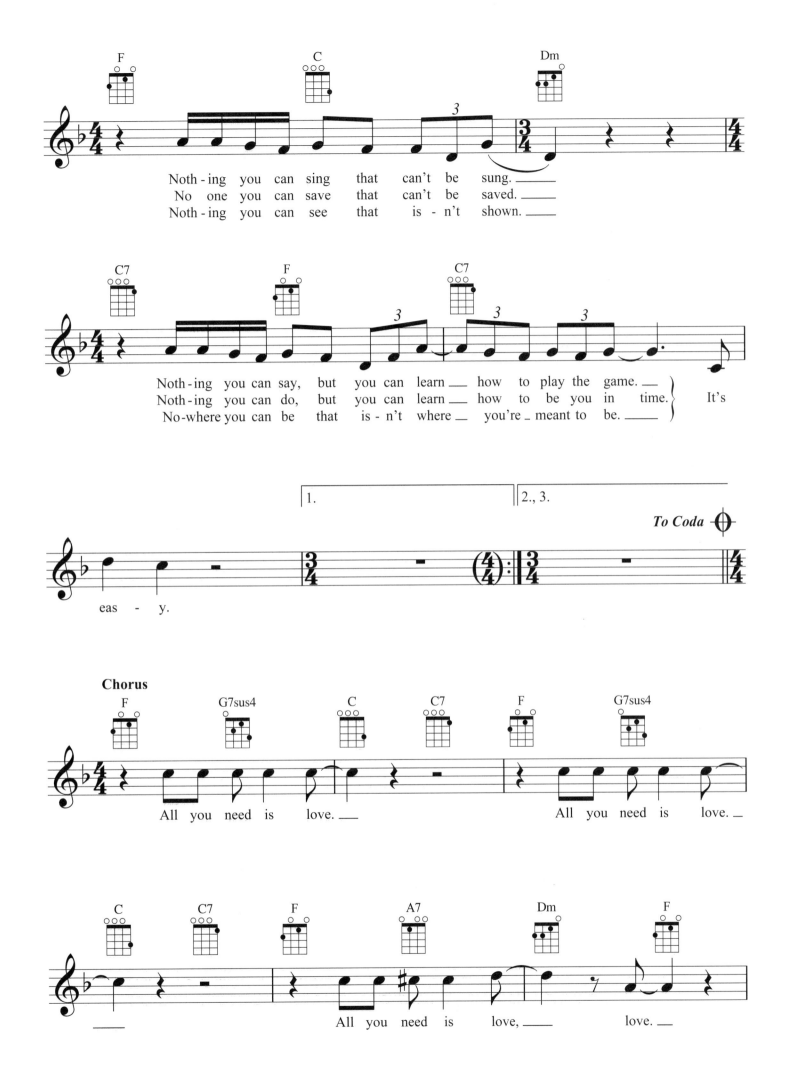

Bless the Beasts and Children

from BLESS THE BEASTS AND CHILDREN
Words and Music by Barry DeVorzon and Perry Botkin, Jr.

Blowin' in the Wind

Words and Music by Bob Dylan

non - balls __ fly __ be - fore __ they are for -

- ev - er banned? __ The an -

Chorus

- swer, my friend, __ is blow - in' in __ the wind. __

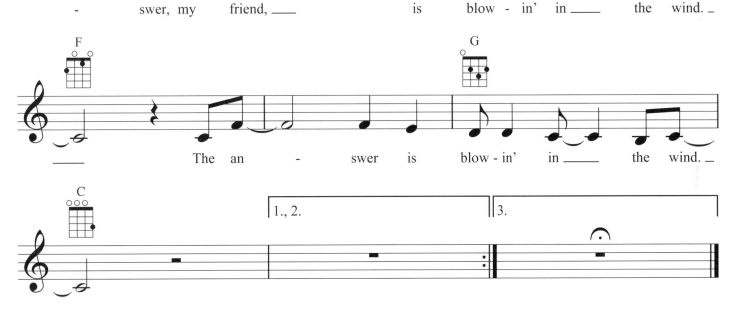

__ The an - swer is blow - in' in __ the wind. __

1., 2.   3.

Additional Lyrics

2. How many years can a mountain exist
   Before it is washed to the sea?
   How many years can some people exist
   Before they're allowed to be free?
   Yes, and how many times can a man turn his head
   And pretend that he just doesn't see?

3. How many times must a man look up
   Before he can see the sky?
   How many ears must one man have
   Before he can hear people cry?
   Yes, and how many deaths will it take till he knows
   That too many people have died?

Bridge Over Troubled Water

Words and Music by Paul Simon

Circle of Life

from Walt Disney Pictures' THE LION KING
Music by Elton John
Lyrics by Tim Rice

find than can ev - er be found. ____ But the
____ "Live and let live." ____ But

all are a - greed ____ as they join the stam - pede, ____ you should
sun roll - ing high ____ through the sap - phi - re sky ____ keeps great and

nev - er take more ___ than you give _____ in the cir - cle of life. __
small on the end - less ___ round _____ in the cir - cle of life. __

Chorus

It's the wheel of for - tune.

It's the leap of faith. ___   It's the band of ___ hope __

____   'til we find ___ our _ place _____

on the path un - wind - ing

in the cir -

- cle, _____

the cir - cle of life. _____

the cir - cle of life! _____

the cir - cle of life. _____

Outro

On the path un-wind ing

in the cir - cle, ___

the cir - cle of life. _____

Candle on the Water

from Walt Disney's PETE'S DRAGON
Words and Music by Al Kasha and Joel Hirschhorn

cir - cling in the air, light - ed by a prayer. _____

Verse

3. I'll be your can - dle on the wa - ter. This flame in - side of me will

grow. Keep hold - ing on; you'll make it. Here's my hand so take it.

Outro

Look for me reach - ing out to show as sure as riv - ers flow,

I'll nev - er let you go. I'll nev - er let you go.

I'll nev - er let you go. _____

Climb Ev'ry Mountain

from THE SOUND OF MUSIC
Lyrics by Oscar Hammerstein II
Music by Richard Rodgers

Everything Is Beautiful

Words and Music by Ray Stevens

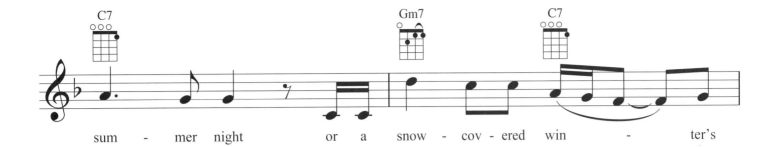

sum - mer night   or a   snow - cov - ered   win -   ter's

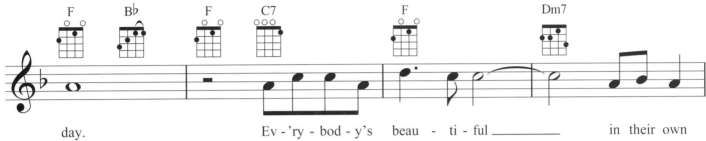

day.   Ev - 'ry - bod - y's beau - ti - ful _____   in their own

way. _____   Un - der God's   heav - en,   the

To Coda ⊕

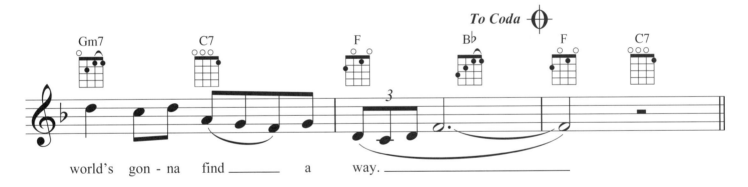

world's gon - na find _____ a   way. _____

Verse

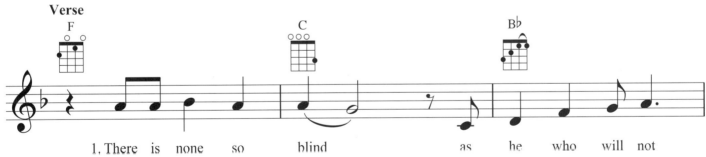

1. There is   none   so   blind   as   he   who   will not
2. *See additional lyrics*

see. _____   We   must not close our   minds, _____   we must

Additional Lyrics

2. We shouldn't care about the length of his hair or the color of his skin.
   Don't worry about what shows from without but the love that lies within.
   We gonna get it all together now and everything's gonna work out fine.
   Just take a little time to look on the good side, my friend, and straighten it out in your mind.

Ebony and Ivory

Words and Music by Paul McCartney

First note

Chorus
Moderately

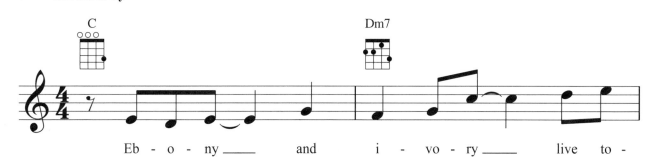

Eb - o - ny _____ and i - vo - ry _____ live to -

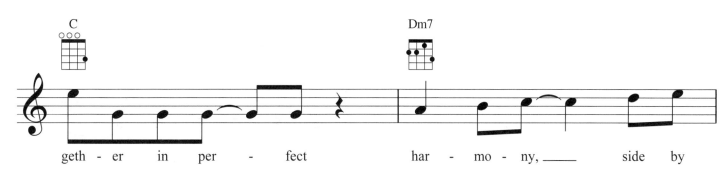

geth - er in per - fect har - mo - ny, _____ side by

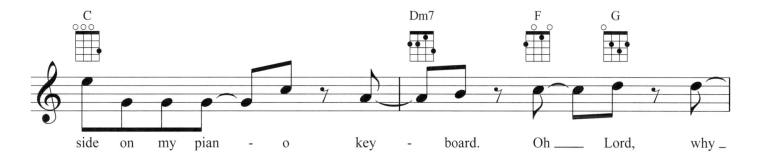

side on my pian - o key - board. Oh _____ Lord, why _

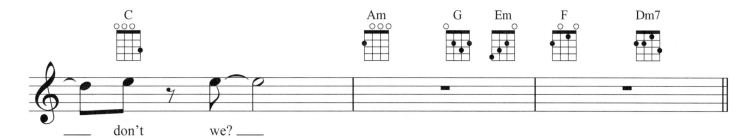

_____ don't we? _____

Verse

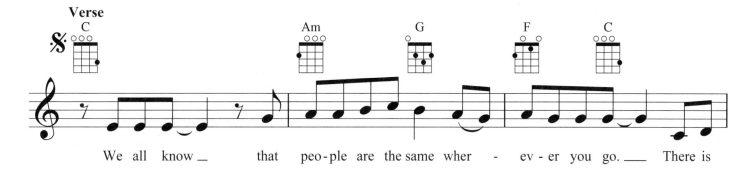

We all know _ that peo - ple are the same wher - ev - er you go. _ There is

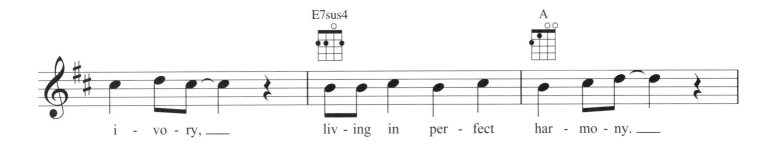

i - vo - ry, ___ liv - ing in per - fect har - mo - ny. ___

Eb - o - ny, ___ i - vo - ry, ___ ooh. ___

D.S. al Coda
(Tempo I)

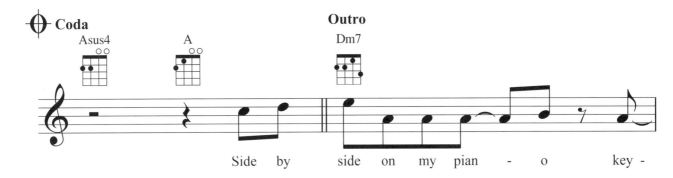

Coda

Outro

Side by side on my pian - o key -

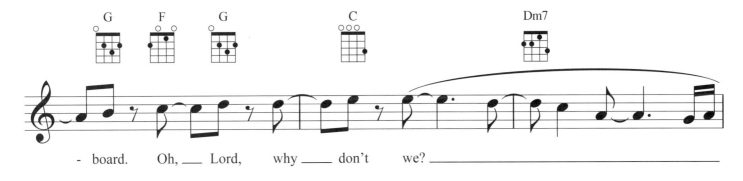

- board. Oh, ___ Lord, why ___ don't we? ___

Double-time

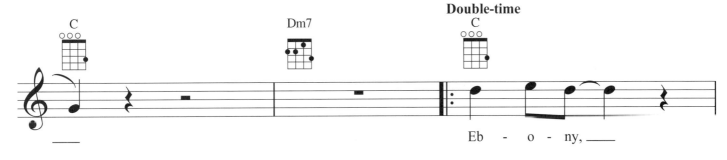

Eb - o - ny, ___

Repeat and fade

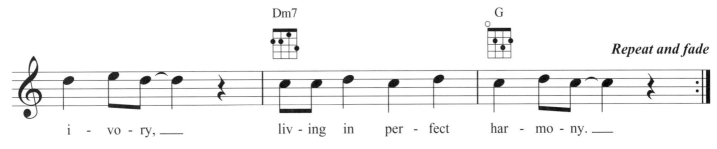

i - vo - ry, ___ liv - ing in per - fect har - mo - ny. ___

27

Friends

Words and Music by Michael W. Smith and Deborah D. Smith

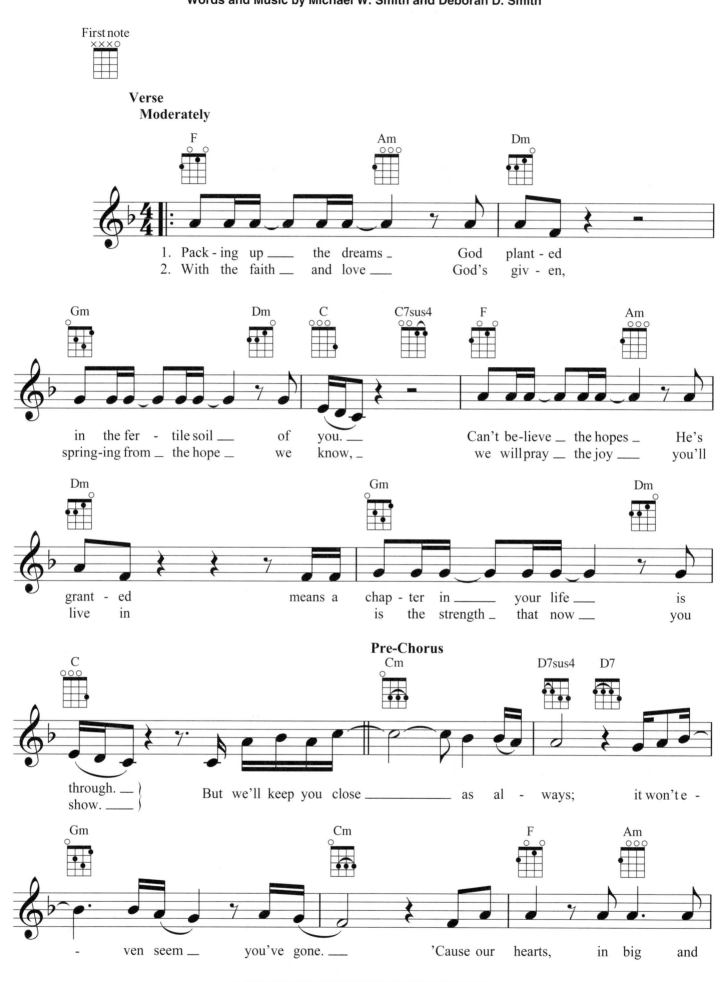

small ways, will keep the love __ that keeps __ us strong.

Chorus

And __ friends are friends __ for - ev - er if the

Lord's the Lord __ of them. __ And a friend will not ___ say "nev - er," 'cause the

wel-come will ___ not end. __ Though it's hard to let ___ you go, ___ in the

Fa - ther's hands _ we know _ that a life - time's not too long __

1. to live _ as friends. __

2.

From a Distance

Words and Music by Julie Gold

song   of ___ ev - 'ry   man. ___   God ___ is

Outro-Bridge

watch - ing   us, ___   God ___ is   watch - ing _____ us,   God ___ is

watch - ing   us   from   a ___   dis - tance. _____   Oh,   God ___ is

watch - ing   us, ___   God ___ is   watch - ing, _____   God ___ is

watch - ing   us _____   from   a   dis - tance.

Let chord ring.

Additional Lyrics

2. From a distance, we all have enough,
   And no one is in need.
   And there are no guns, no bombs and no disease,
   No hungry mouths to feed.

Chorus: From a distance, we are instruments,
   Marching in a common band,
   Playing songs of hope, playing songs of peace.
   They're the songs of ev'ry man.

3. From a distance, you look like my friend,
   Even though we are at war.
   From a distance, I just cannot comprehend
   What all this fighting is for.

Chorus: From a distance, there is harmony,
   And it echoes through the land.
   It's the hope of hopes, it's the love of loves,
   It's the heart of ev'ry man.

The Greatest Love of All

Words by Linda Creed
Music by Michael Masser

never to walk in an - y-one's shad-ow. If I fail, ___ if I suc-ceed, ___ at

least I lived ___ as I be - lieve. No mat - ter what they take from me, they

can't take a - way my dig - ni - ty. Be - cause the

Chorus

great - est love of all ___ is hap - pen - ing to

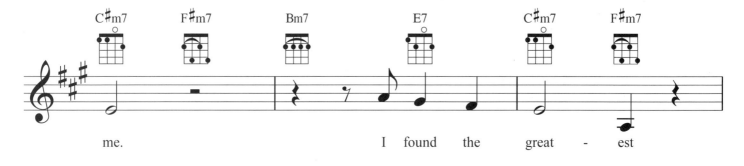

me. I found the great - est

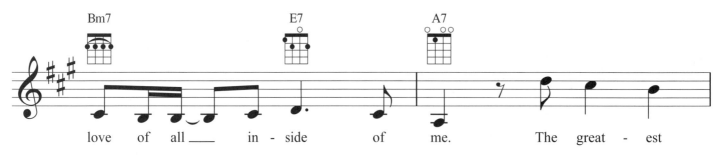

love of all ___ in - side of me. The great - est

He Ain't Heavy, He's My Brother

Words and Music by Bob Russell and Bobby Scott

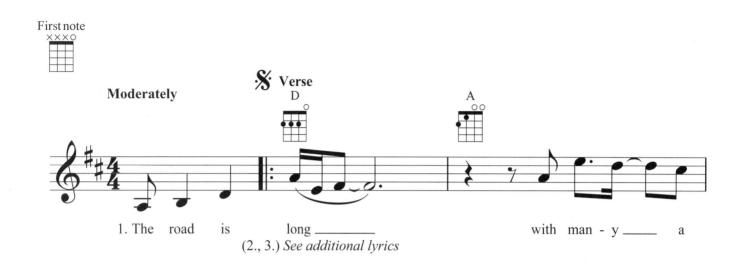

1. The road is long _____ with man-y ____ a
(2., 3.) *See additional lyrics*

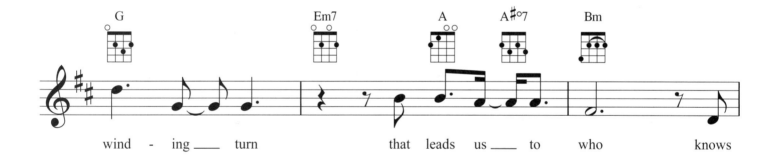

wind - ing ____ turn that leads us ____ to who knows

where, who knows ____ where. _____ But I'm

strong, _____ strong e - nough to car - ry

him.   He ain't heav - y, _____ he's my

broth - er. _____ 2. So on we If I'm

Bridge

lad - en   at all, _____ I'm __

lad - en   with sad - ness __ that ev - 'ry - one's __

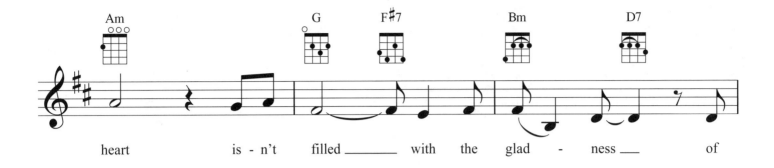

heart   is - n't   filled _____ with   the   glad -   ness ____   of

love   for   one ____ an - oth - er. ____

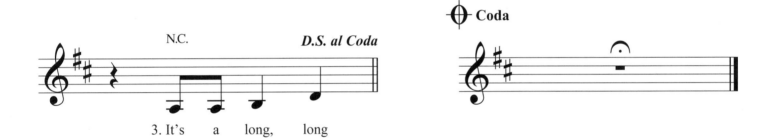

3. It's   a   long,   long

Additional Lyrics

2. So on we go;
   His welfare is of my concern.
   No burden is he to bear;
   We'll get there.
   For I know
   He would not encumber me.
   He ain't heavy, he's my brother.

3. It's a long, long road,
   From which there is no return.
   While we're on the way to there,
   Why not share?
   And the load
   Doesn't weigh me down at all.
   He ain't heavy, he's my brother.

Heal the World

Written and Composed by Michael Jackson

40

I'd Like to Teach the World to Sing

Words and Music by Bill Backer, Roquel Davis, Roger Cook and Roger Greenaway

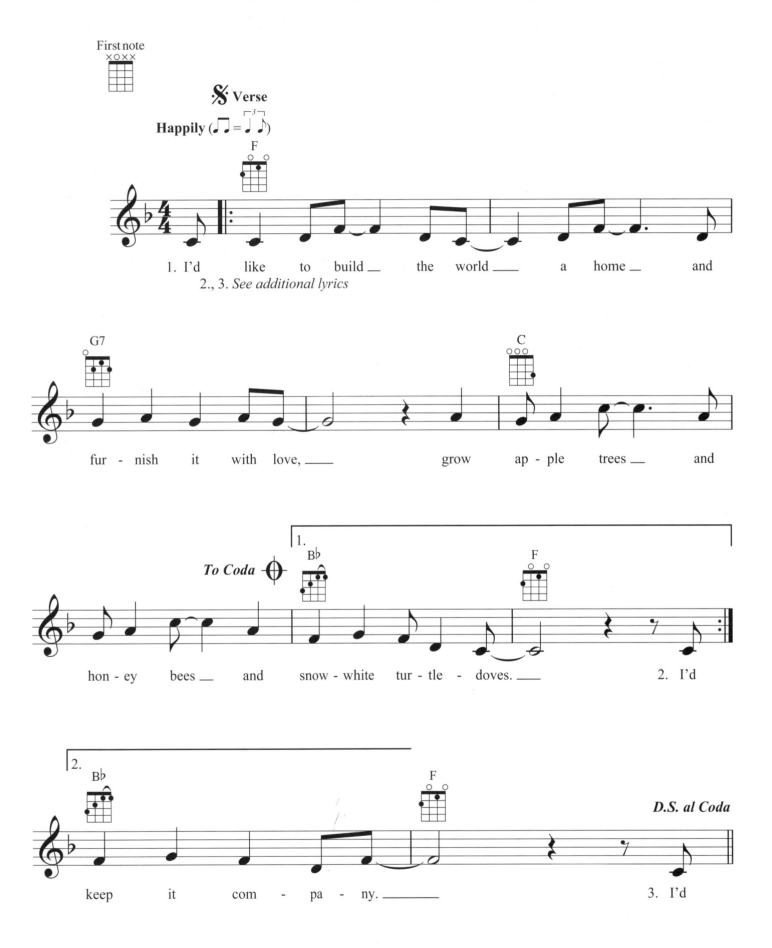

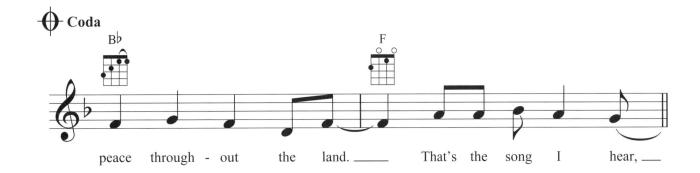

Coda

peace through - out the land. _____ That's the song I hear, ___

Bridge

_____ let the world sing to - day.

Outro

I'd like to teach ___ the world ___ to sing ___ in

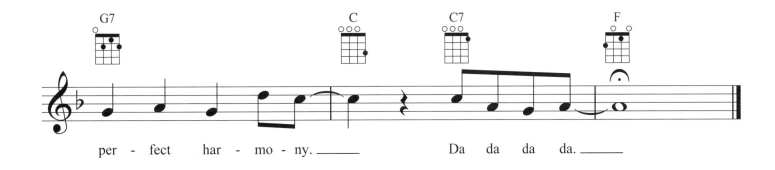

per - fect har - mo - ny. _____ Da da da da. _____

Additional Lyrics

2. I'd like to teach the world to sing in perfect harmony.
   I'd like to hold it in my arms and keep it company.

3. I'd like to see the world, for once, all standing hand in hand,
   And hear them echo through the hills for peace throughout the land.

If I Can Dream

Words and Music by W. Earl Brown

why? _____ 2. There must be why __ won't that sun ap-

Bridge

pear? _____ We're lost in a cloud __

with too much rain. _____ We're trapped in a world __

that's trou-bled with pain. _____ But as long as a man has __ the

strength to __ dream, __ he can re-deem his soul _____ and

fly. _____ He can fly. _____ 3. Deep in my

If I Ruled the World

from PICKWICK

Words by Leslie Bricusse
Music by Cyril Ornadel

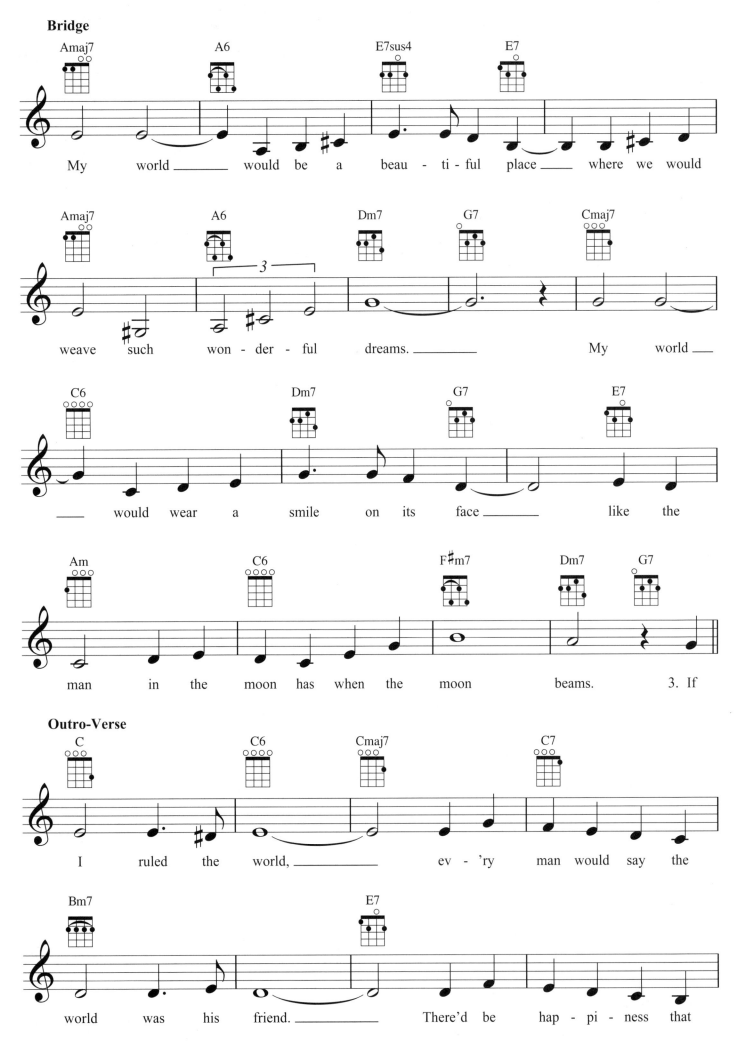

Bridge

My world _____ would be a beau - ti - ful place _____ where we would

weave such won - der - ful dreams. _____ My world _____

_____ would wear a smile on its face _____ like the

man in the moon has when the moon beams. 3. If

Outro-Verse

I ruled the world, _____ ev - 'ry man would say the

world was his friend. _____ There'd be hap - pi - ness that

If I Had a Hammer

(The Hammer Song)

Words and Music by Lee Hays and Pete Seeger

love be - tween my broth - ers and my sis - ters,

all _____ o - ver this

1.–3.

land.

2., 3. If I had a
4. Well, I got a

4.

land. _____

Additional Lyrics

2. If I had a bell, I'd ring it in the morning,
   I'd ring it in the evening all over this land.
   I'd ring out danger, I'd ring out a warning,
   I'd ring out love between my brothers and my sisters,
   All over this land.

3. If I had a song, I'd sing it in the morning,
   I'd sing it in the evening all over this land.
   I'd sing out danger, I'd sing out a warning,
   I'd sing out love between my brothers and my sisters,
   All over this land.

4. Well, I got a hammer, and I've got a bell,
   And I've got a song to sing all over this land.
   It's the hammer of justice, it's the bell of freedom,
   It's the song about love between my brothers and my sisters,
   All over this land.

If We Only Have Love
(Quand on n'a que l'amour)
from JACQUES BREL IS ALIVE AND WELL AND LIVING IN PARIS

French Words and Music by Jacques Brel
English Words by Mort Shuman and Eric Blau

Bridge

Imagine

Written by John Lennon

First note

Intro
Moderately slow

(Instrumental)

Verse

1. I - mag - ine there's   no   heav - en,   it's eas - y   if   you   try; _____

_____   no   hell _____   be - low   us,

a - bove us   on - ly   sky. _____   I - mag - ine all   the peo -

ple _____   liv - ing   for to - day, _____   ah. _____

Verse

— 2. I - mag - ine there's no coun - tries,
3. *See additional lyrics*

it is - n't hard ___ to do; ___

noth - ing to kill or die ___ for

and no re - li - gion, too. ___

I - mag - ine all the peo - ple ___

liv - ing life in peace. ___ You, ___

Chorus

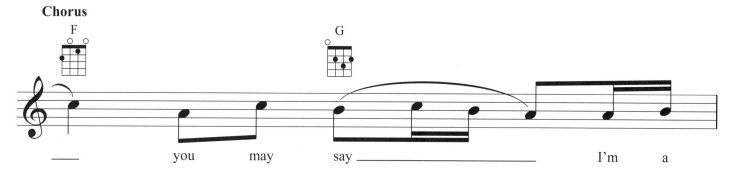

you may say _____ I'm a

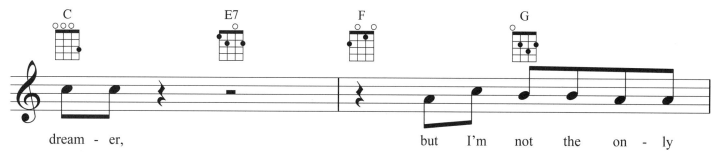

dream - er, but I'm not the on - ly

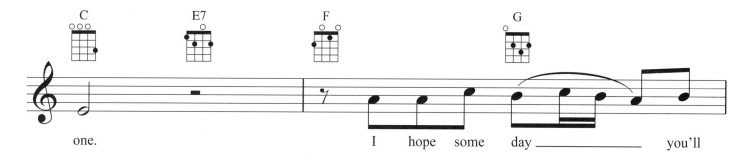

one. I hope some day _____ you'll

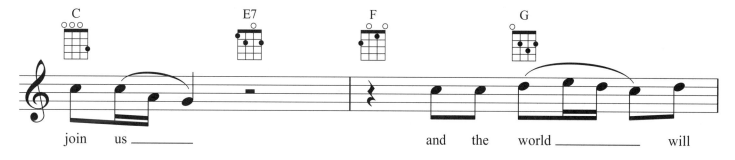

join us _____ and the world _____ will

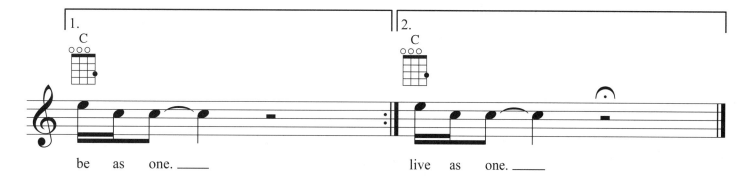

1.
be as one. ____

2.
live as one. ____

Additional Lyrics

3. Imagine no possessions,
   I wonder if you can;
   No need for greed or hunger,
   A brotherhood of man.
   Imagine all the people sharing all the world.

The Impossible Dream
(The Quest)

from MAN OF LA MANCHA

Lyric by Joe Darion
Music by Mitch Leigh

right _____ with - out ques - tion or pause, _____ to be will - ing to

march in - to hell for a heav - en - ly cause! And I

know, _____ if I'll on - ly be true _____ to this glo - ri - ous

quest, _____ that my heart _____ will lie peace-ful and calm, _____ when I'm laid to my

D.S. al Coda

rest. 3. And the

Coda

cour - age, _____ to

reach _____ the un - reach - a - ble stars. _____

Last Night I Had the Strangest Dream

Words and Music by Ed McCurdy

First note

Moderately   Verse

1. Last   night   I   had   the
(2.) when   the   pa   -   per
(3.) night   I   had   the

strang - est   dream   I'd   ev - er
was   all   signed   and a   mil - lion
strang - est   dream   I'd   ev - er

dreamed   be - fore. _____   I
cop - ies   made, _____   they
dreamed   be - fore. _____   I

dreamed   the   world   had   all   a -
all   joined   hands   and   bowed   their
dreamed   the   world   had   all   a -

To Coda

greed   to   put   an   end   to
heads,   and   put   grate - ful   prayers   were
greed   to   put   an   end   to

Lean on Me

Words and Music by Bill Withers

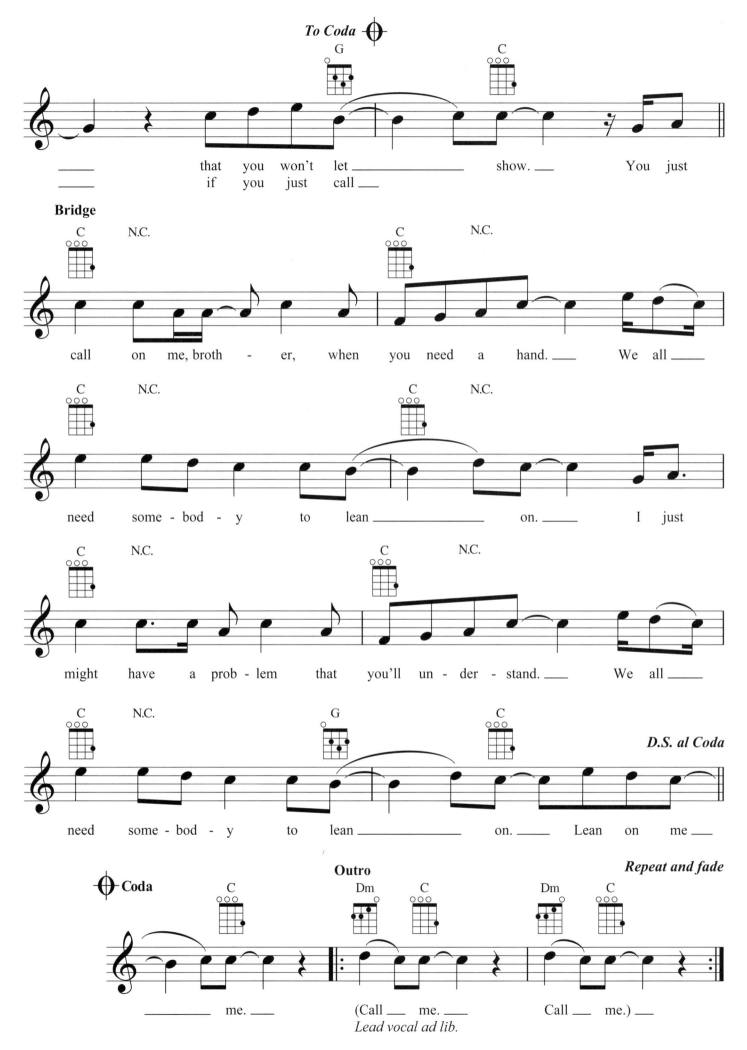

Let It Be

Words and Music by John Lennon and Paul McCartney

Chorus

be. ⟩ / be. ⟩

Let it be, _____ let it be, _____ let it be, _

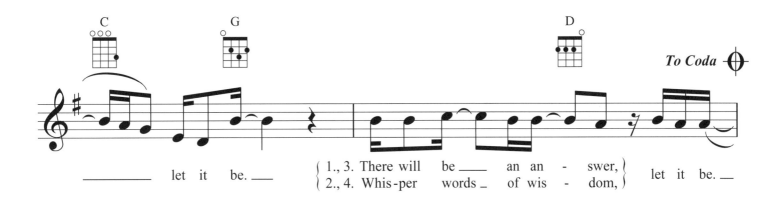

To Coda

_____ let it be. _ { 1., 3. There will be _ an an - swer, } { 2., 4. Whis-per words _ of wis - dom, } let it be. _

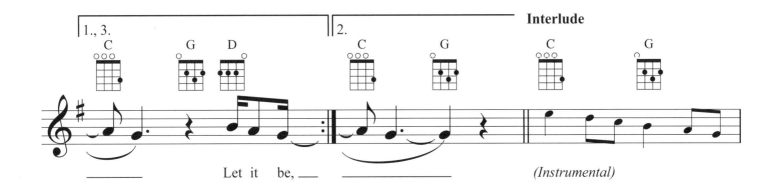

Interlude

1., 3. | 2.

_____ Let it be, _ _____ *(Instrumental)*

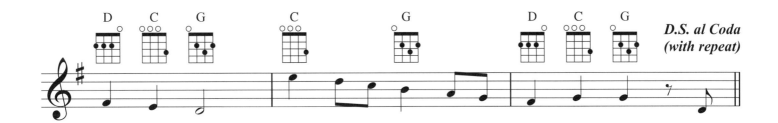

D.S. al Coda (with repeat)

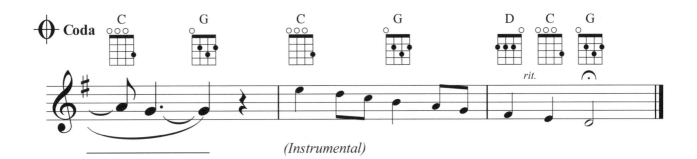

⊕ **Coda**

rit.

_____ *(Instrumental)*

Let There Be Peace on Earth

Words and Music by Sy Miller and Jill Jackson

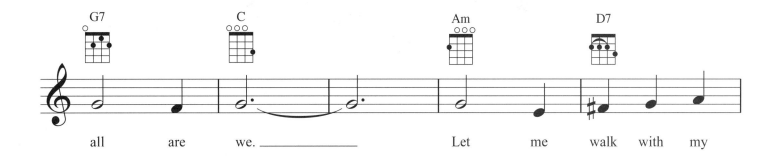

all are we. _____ Let me walk with my

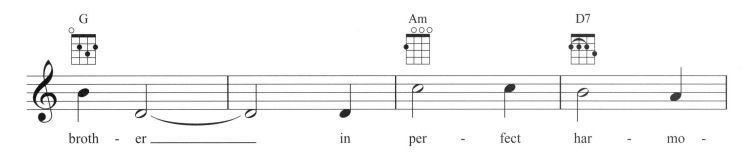

broth - er _____ in per - fect har - mo -

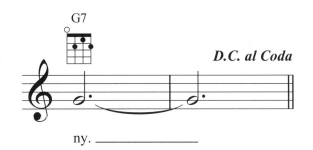

D.C. al Coda

ny. _____

Outro
Coda

take each mo - ment and

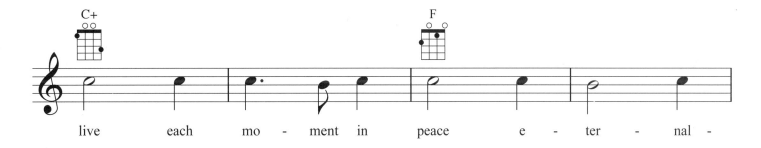

live each mo - ment in peace e - ter - nal -

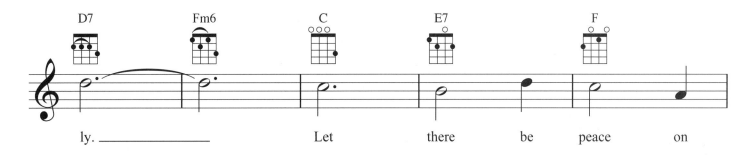

ly. _____ Let there be peace on

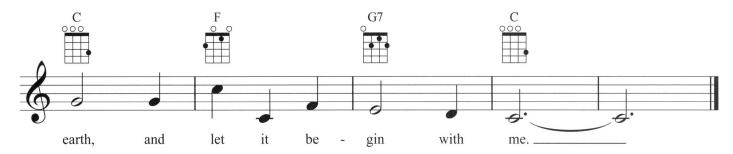

earth, and let it be - gin with me. _____

69

Let's Get Together

(Get Together)

Words and Music by Chet Powers

1. Love is but the song we sing, and fear's the way we die.
2. Some will come and some will go, and we shall sure-ly pass.
3. If you heard the song I sing, you must un-der-stand.

You can make the moun-tains ring, or make the an-gels cry.
When the one who left us here re-turns for us at last,
You hold the key to love and fear all in your trem-bling hand.

Know the dove is on the wing, _____ and
we are but a mo - ment's sun - light
One key _____ un - locks them both you know and

you need not _____ know why. _____
fad - ing on the grass. _____
it's at your _____ com - mand. _____

Chorus

Come on, peo - ple now, smile on your broth - er. Ev - 'ry -

bod - y get to - geth - er, try and love one an - oth - er right _____

1., 2.

To Coda

3.

D.S. al Coda

now. _____

CODA

Right _____ now! Right _____ now!

Lonely People

Words and Music by Dan Peek and Catherine L. Peek

Lost in the Stars

from the Musical Production LOST IN THE STARS
Words by Maxwell Anderson
Music by Kurt Weill

Love Will Be Our Home

Words and Music by Steven Curtis Chapman

Love Can Build a Bridge

Words and Music by Paul Overstreet, John Jarvis and Naomi Judd

Over the Rainbow

from THE WIZARD OF OZ
Music by Harold Arlen
Lyric by E.Y. "Yip" Harburg

People Got to Be Free

Words and Music by Felix Cavaliere and Edward Brigati, Jr.

First note

Chorus
Moderately

All the world o - ver, it's so eas - y to see; __ peo - ple ev - 'ry - where just

wan - na be free. __

Lis - ten, please, lis - ten; that's the way it should be. __
Can't un - der - stand, it's so sim - ple to me, __

Peace in the val - ley, peo - ple got to be free. _____
peo - ple ev - 'ry - where just got to be free. _____

Verse

1. You should see __
2. If there's a man __

_____ what a love - ly, love - ly world this would be _____
_____ who is down and needs a help - ing hand, _____ all it

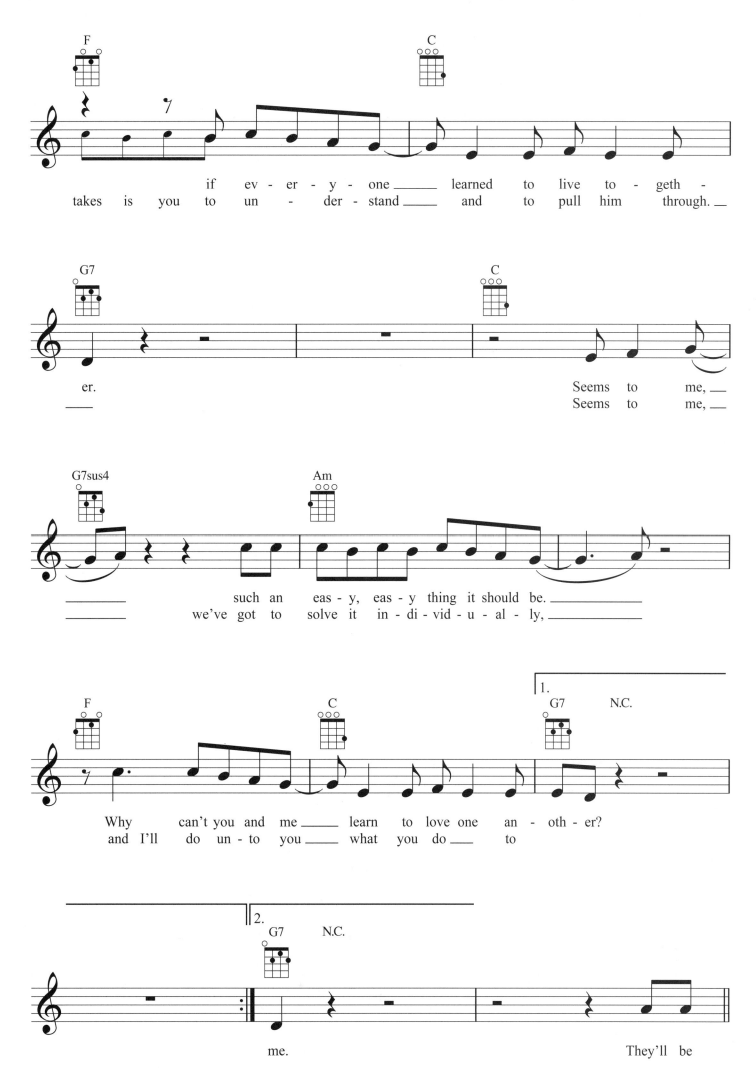

Outro-Chorus

shout - in' from the moun - tain on   out   to   the   sea. ____
Oh, ____ what a feel - in' just come o - ver me; ____ it's e -

No two ways a - bout it; peo - ple have to be free. ____
nough to move a moun - tain, make a blind ____ man see. ____

Ask me my o - pin - ion, my o - pin - ion will be: ____ it's a
Ev - 'ry - bod - y's danc - in'; come on, let's ____ go see. ____ There's

nat - 'ral sit - u - a - tion for a man to be free. ____
peace ____ in the val - ley, now we all can be free. ____

Peace Train

Words and Music by Cat Stevens

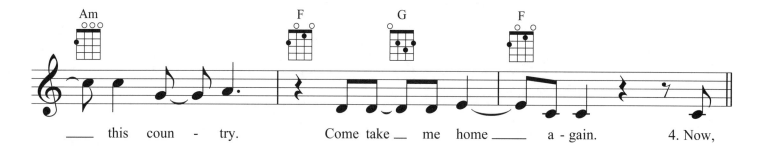

this coun - try. Come take __ me home __ a - gain. 4. Now,

Verse

I've been __ smil - in' late - ly, __ think-in' a - bout __ the good things

6., 8. *See additional lyrics*

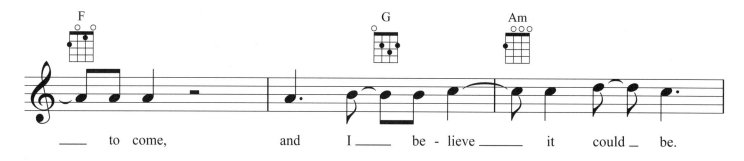

__ to come, and I __ be - lieve __ it could __ be.

Chorus

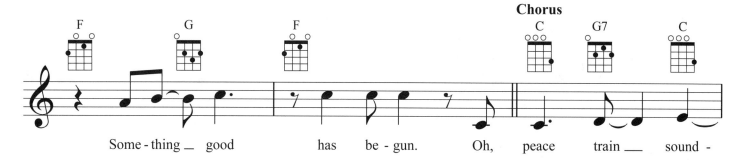

Some - thing __ good has be - gun. Oh, peace train __ sound -

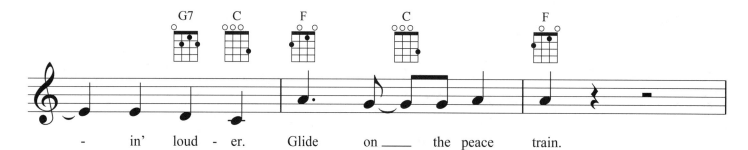

- in' loud - er. Glide on __ the peace train.

To Coda 1

Come on __ the peace train.

Peace train, — ho - ly roll - er, ev - 'ry-one jump — up on the peace train.

Come on — now, peace

To Coda 2

D.S. al Coda 1

train.

Coda 1

D.S. al Coda 2

train. 7. Now,

Coda 2

train.

Outro

Come on, _____ peace _____

_____ train. Yes, it's ___ the peace train.

Additional Lyrics

5. Get your bags together.
   Go bring your good friends, too.
   Because it's gettin' nearer.
   It soon will be with you.

6. Oh, come and join the living;
   It's not so far from you,
   And it's gettin' nearer.
   Soon it will all be true.

7. Now, I've been cryin' lately,
   Thinkin' about the world as it is.
   Why must we go on hating?
   Why can't we live in bliss?

8. 'Cause out on the edge of darkness,
   There rides a peace train.
   Oh, peace train, take this country.
   Come take me home again.

Put a Little Love in Your Heart

Words and Music by Jimmy Holiday, Randy Myers and Jackie DeShannon

G   Am   D

____   will   be   a   bet-ter   place   for   you ____

____   and   me. ____   You   just   wait ____

1., 2.   ____   and   see. ____   3.   ____   and   see.

Outro

C   G   *Repeat and fade*

Put   a   lit-tle   love   in   your   heart. _____

Additional Lyrics

2. Another day goes by, and still the children cry.
   Put a little love in your heart.
   If you want the world to know we won't let hatred grow,
   Put a little love in your heart.

3. Take a good look around, and if you're lookin' down,
   Put a little love in your heart.
   I hope when you decide, kindness will be your guide.
   Put a little love in your heart.

The Rainbow Connection

from THE MUPPET MOVIE

Words and Music by Paul Williams and Kenneth L. Ascher

spell, we know that it's prob - a - bly mag - ic.

Coda
Outro

me. La da da dee da da do la

la da da da de da do.

Additional Lyrics

2. Who said that ev'ry wish would be heard and answered
   When wished on the morning star?
   Somebody thought of that and someone believed it;
   Look what it's done so far.
   What's so amazing that keeps us stargazing,
   And what do we think we might see?

3. Have you been half asleep and have you heard voices?
   I've heard them calling my name.
   Is this the sweet sound that calls the young sailors?
   The voice might be one and the same.
   I've heard it too many times to ignore it;
   It's something that I'm s'posed to be.

Seasons of Love

from RENT
Words and Music by Jonathan Larson

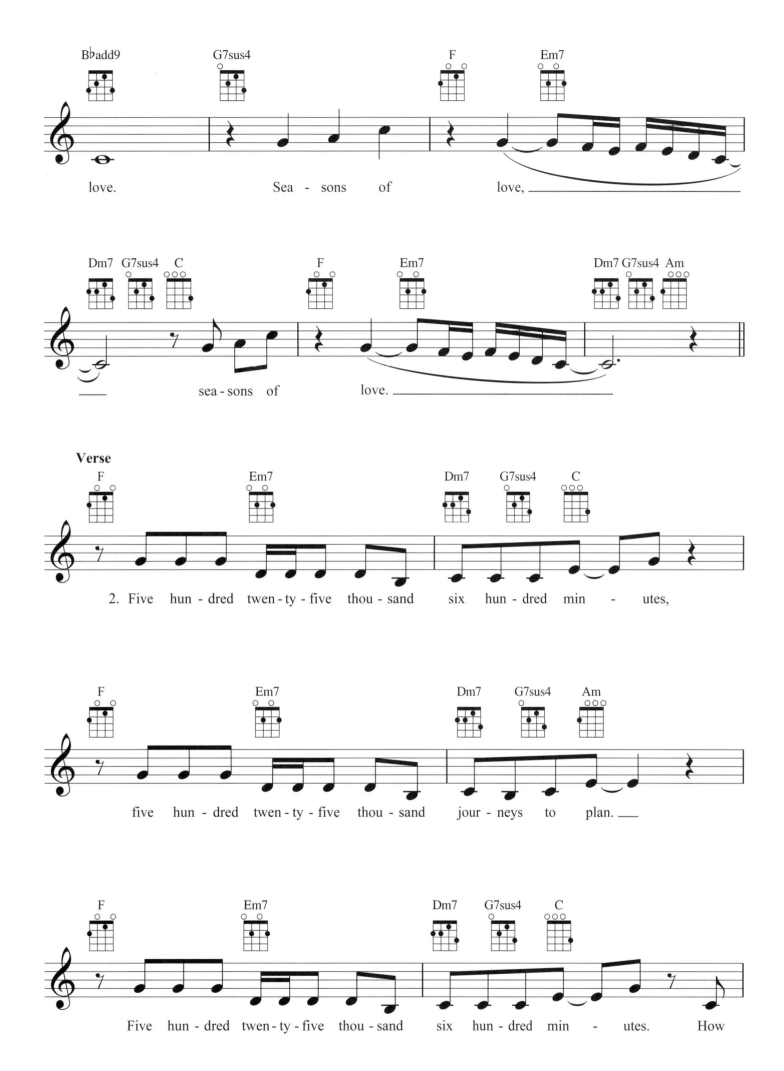

Chorus

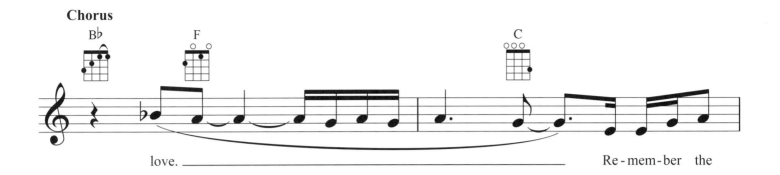

love. _____ Re - mem - ber the

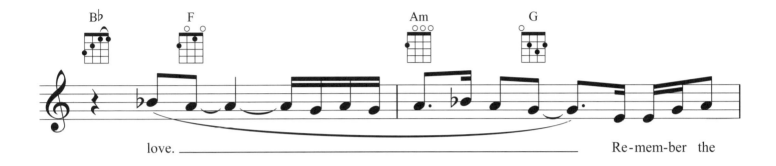

love. _____ Re - mem - ber the

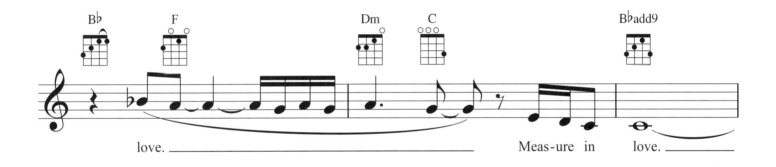

love. _____ Meas - ure in love. _____

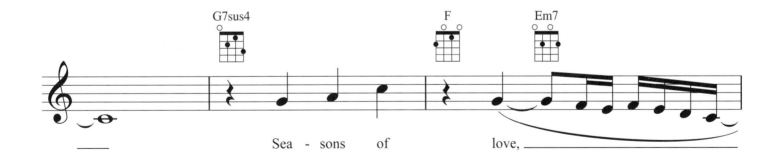

___ Sea - sons of love, _____

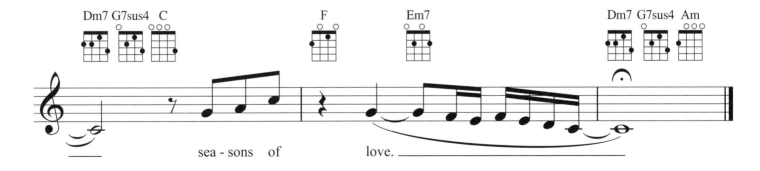

___ sea - sons of love. _____

Reach Out and Touch
(Somebody's Hand)
Words and Music by Nickolas Ashford and Valerie Simpson

The Rose

from the Twentieth Century-Fox Motion Picture Release THE ROSE
Words and Music by Amanda McBroom

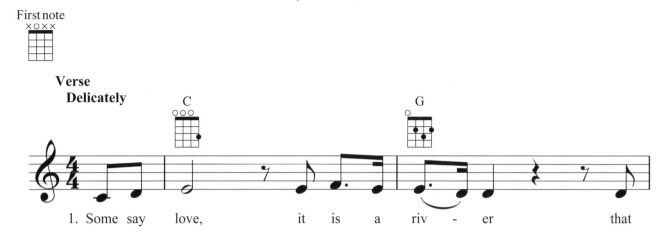

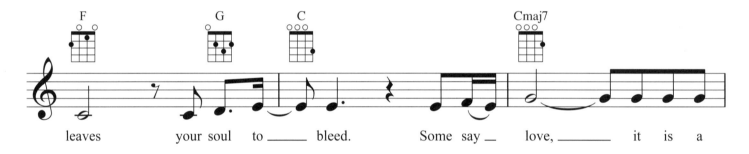

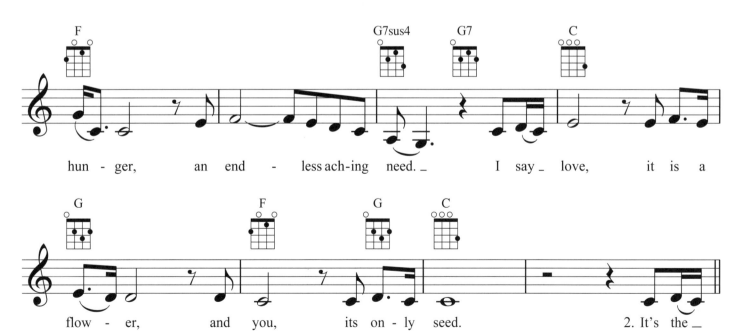

Verse

heart a - fraid of break - ing that nev - er _____ learns to
(3.) night has been too lone - ly and the road _____ has been too

dance. It's the __ dream _____ a - fraid of wak - ing that
long, and you __ think _____ that love is on - ly for the

nev - er _____ takes the _____ chance. It's the __ one _____ who won't
luck - y _____ and the _____ strong, just re - mem - ber in the

be tak - en, _____ who can - not seem to give, __ and the __
win - ter far be - neath _____ the bit - ter snows lies the __

soul a - fraid of dy - ing that nev - er _____ learns to
seed that with the sun's love in the

live.   3. When the __ spring be - comes the rose.

Sing

from SESAME STREET
Words and Music by Joe Raposo

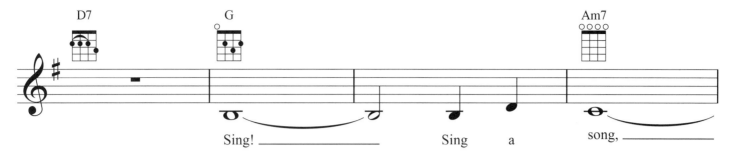

D7   G   Am7

Sing! _____ Sing a song, _____

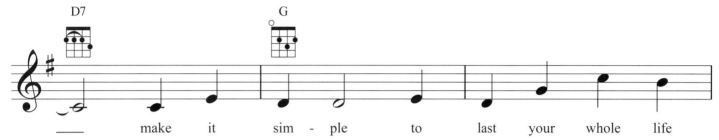

D7   G

_____ make it sim - ple to last your whole life

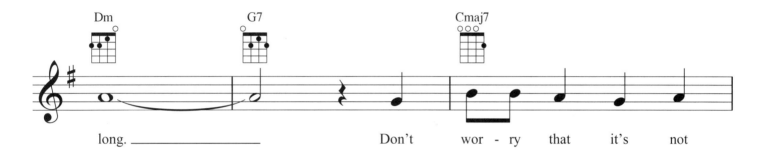

Dm   G7   Cmaj7

long. _____ Don't wor - ry that it's not

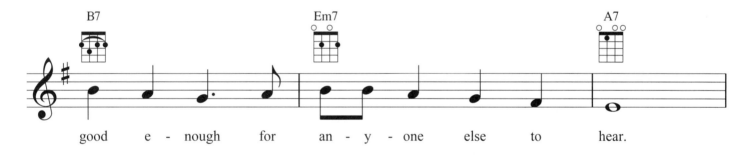

B7   Em7   A7

good e - nough for an - y - one else to hear.

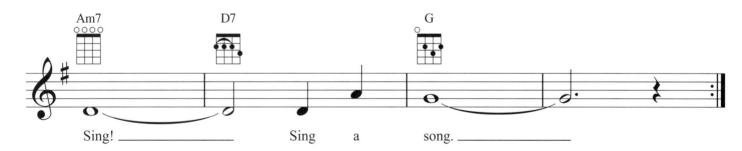

Am7   D7   G

Sing! _____ Sing a song. _____

Outro

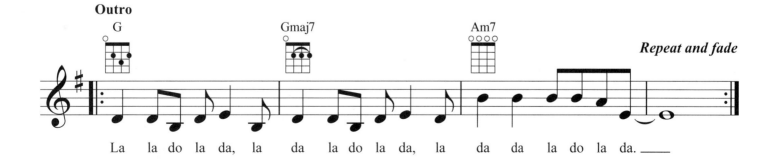

G   Gmaj7   Am7   *Repeat and fade*

La la do la da, la da la do la da, la da da la do la da. ____

Somewhere Out There

from AN AMERICAN TAIL

Music by Barry Mann and James Horner
Lyric by Cynthia Weil

far a-part we are, it helps to think we might be wish-in'

on the same bright star. And when the night wind starts to sing that

lone-some ___ lull-a-by, it helps to think we're sleep-ing un-der-

Outro-Verse

neath the same big sky. Some-where out there, if

love can see us through, then we'll be to-geth-er some-where

out there, out where dreams come true. _____

107

Tears in Heaven

Words and Music by Eric Clapton and Will Jennings

First note

Verse
Moderate, relaxed tempo

1. Would you know   my   name _____
2. Would you hold   my   hand _____
3. Would you know   my   name _____

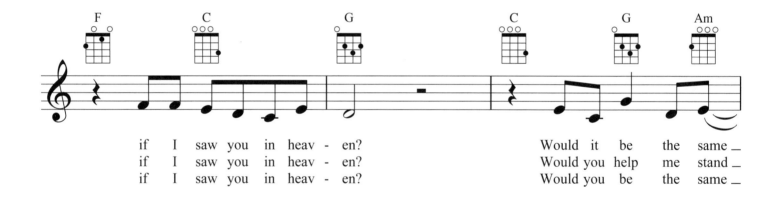

if I saw you in heav - en?   Would it be   the   same _
if I saw you in heav - en?   Would you help me   stand _
if I saw you in heav - en?   Would you be   the   same _

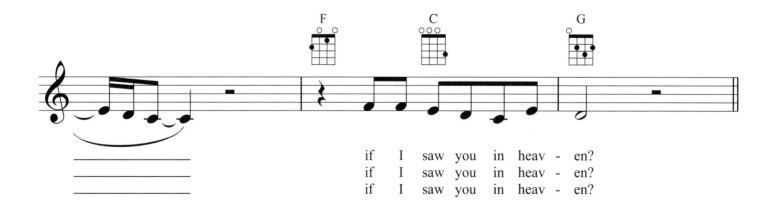

_____   if I saw you in heav - en?
_____   if I saw you in heav - en?
_____   if I saw you in heav - en?

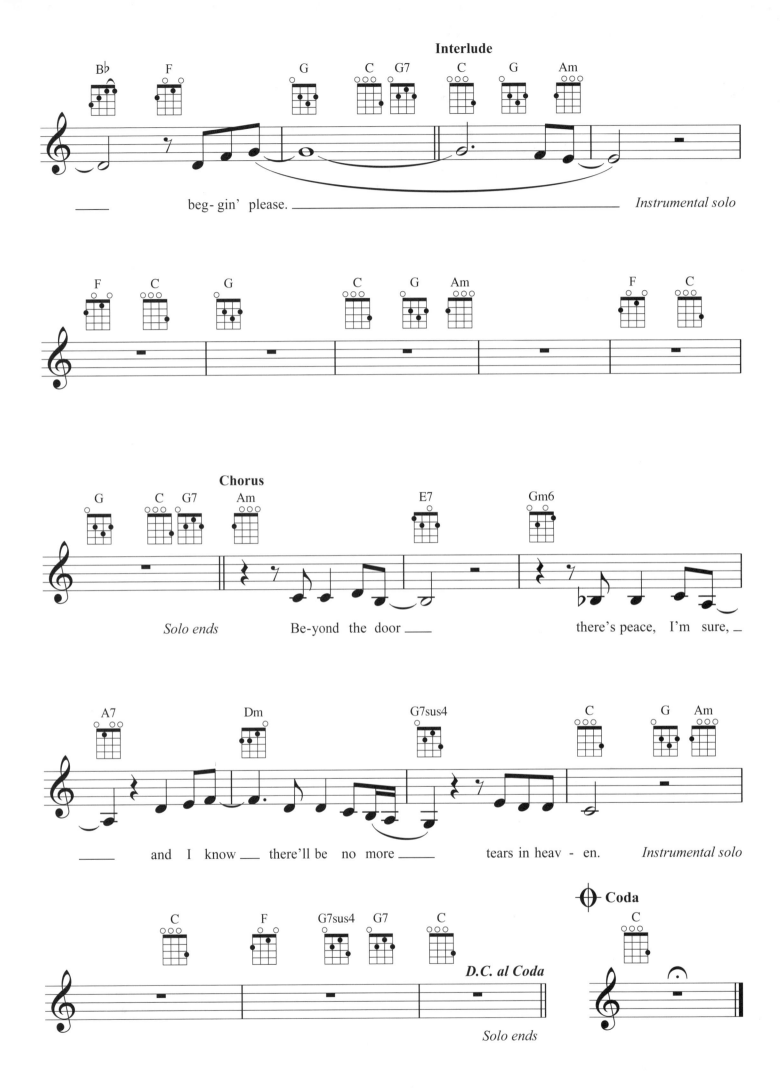

Interlude

_____ beg- gin' please. _____ *Instrumental solo*

Solo ends   Be-yond the door _____   there's peace, I'm sure, _

Chorus

_____ and I know ___ there'll be no more _____ tears in heav - en.   *Instrumental solo*

D.C. al Coda

Coda

Solo ends

110

Shower the People

Words and Music by James Taylor

oth - er; _____ it does-n't take an - y sac - ri - fice. _
way that you feel, you can feel it be - gin - ning to ease. _

_____ Oh, _____ fa - ther and moth - er, sis -
_____ I think it's true what they say a - bout the

ter and broth - er, if it feels nice _____ don't _____
squeak - y wheel, _____ al - ways get - ting the grease. _

Chorus

_____ think twice. _ Just } show - er the peo - ple you love _
_____ Bet - ter _____ to }

_____ with love; _____ show them the way _____ that you feel. _

Things are gon - na { work out / be just } fine _____ if you on - ly will. _

112

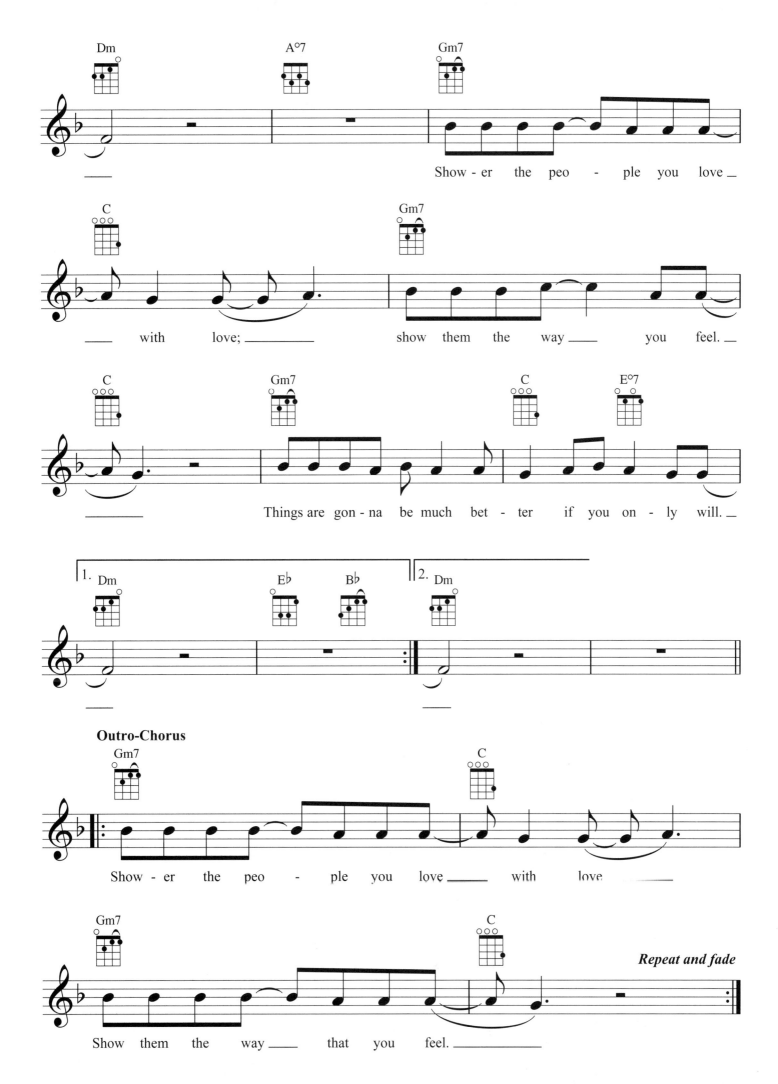

Show-er the peo - ple you love _

_ with love; _____ show them the way ___ you feel. _

_____ Things are gon - na be much bet - ter if you on - ly will. _

Outro-Chorus

Show-er the peo - ple you love _____ with love. _____

Repeat and fade

Show them the way ___ that you feel. _____

That's What Friends Are For

Music by Burt Bacharach
Words by Carole Bayer Sager

Tomorrow

from the Musical Production ANNIE

Lyric by Martin Charnin
Music by Charles Strouse

Chorus

Outro

Touch the Hand of Love

Words by Mahriah Blackwolf
Music by Blossom Dearie

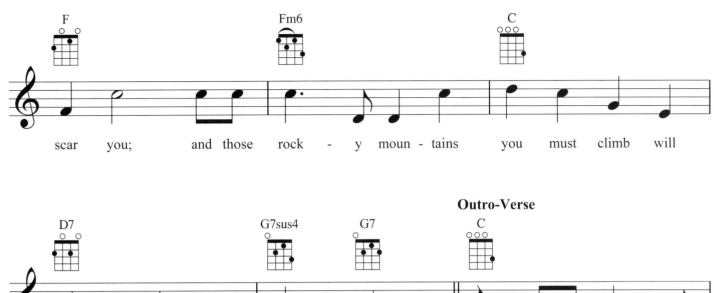

scar you; and those rock - y moun - tains you must climb will

Outro-Verse

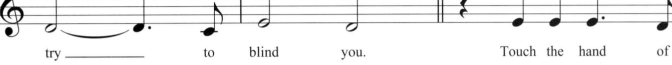

try _____ to blind you. Touch the hand of

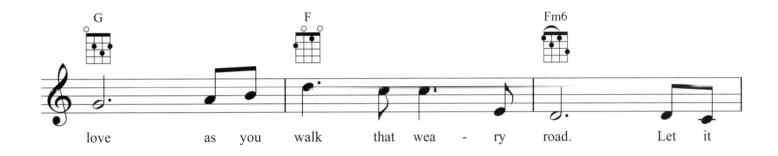

love as you walk that wea - ry road. Let it

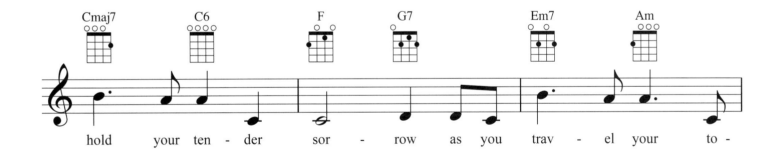

hold your ten - der sor - row as you trav - el your to -

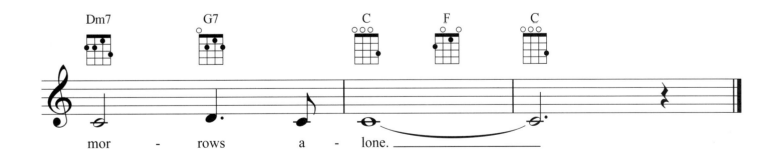

mor - rows a - lone. _____

True Colors

Words and Music by Billy Steinberg and Tom Kelly

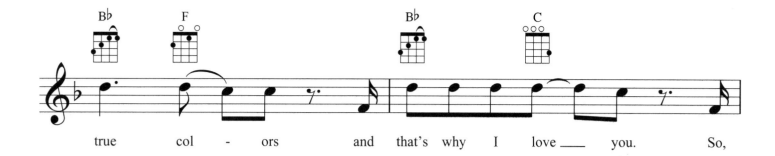

true col - ors and that's why I love ____ you. So,

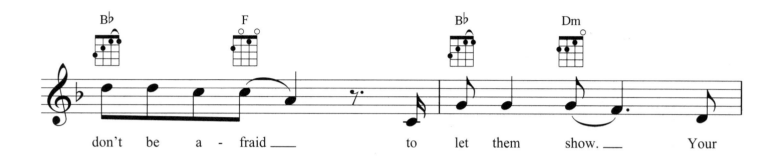

don't be a - fraid ____ to let them show. ____ Your

To Coda ⊕

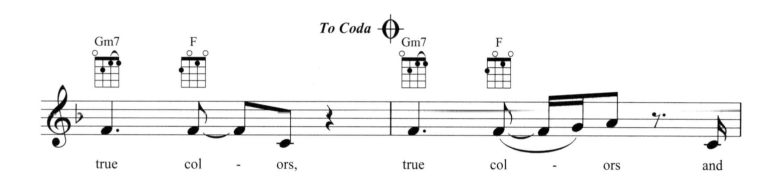

true col - ors, true col - ors and

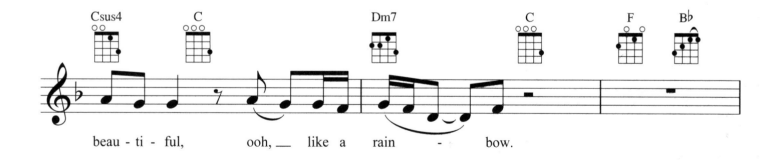

beau - ti - ful, ooh, ____ like a rain - bow.

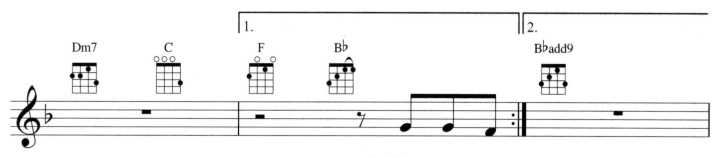

2. Show me your

Outro-Chorus

- in' through.   I   see   your   true   col - ors   and

that's   why   I   love ____   you.   So,   don't   be   a - fraid, ____   just

let   them ____   show. ____   Your   true   col - ors,

true   col - ors,   true ____   col - ors   are   beau - ti - ful,

beau - ti - ful   like   a   rain - bow.

Turn! Turn! Turn!
(To Everything There Is a Season)

Words from the Book of Ecclesiastes
Adaptation and Music by Pete Seeger

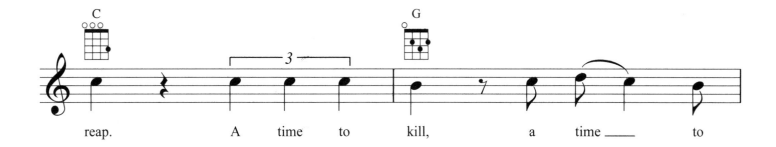

reap.   A   time   to   kill,   a   time __ to

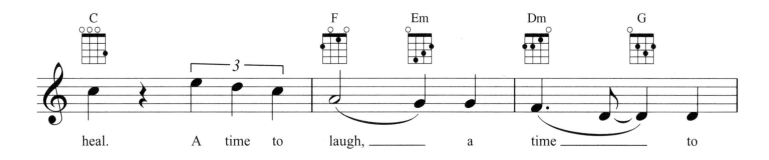

heal.   A   time   to   laugh, ___ a   time ____ to

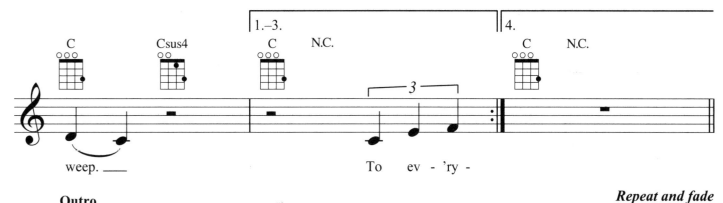

weep. __   To   ev - 'ry -

Outro   *Repeat and fade*

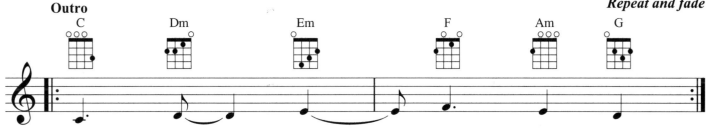

(Instrumental)

Additional Lyrics

2. A time to build up, a time to break down.
   A time to dance, a time to mourn.
   A time to cast away stones,
   A time to gather stones together.

3. A time of love, a time of hate.
   A time of war, a time of peace.
   A time you may embrace,
   A time to refrain from embracing.

4. A time to gain, a time to lose.
   A time to rend, a time to sew.
   A time for love, a time for hate.
   A time for peace; I swear it's not too late.

What a Wonderful World

Words and Music by George David Weiss and Bob Thiele

We Are the World

Words and Music by Lionel Richie and Michael Jackson

1. There comes a time ___ when we heed a cer - tain call, ___
2., 3. *See additional lyrics*

___ when the world must come to - geth - er as

one. There are peo - ple dy - ing,

oh, and it's time ___ to lend a hand to life, ___

___ the great - est gift ___ of all.

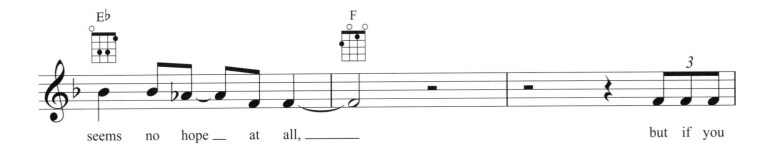

seems no hope __ at all, _____ but if you

just be - lieve, __ there's no way we can fall. _____ Well, well,

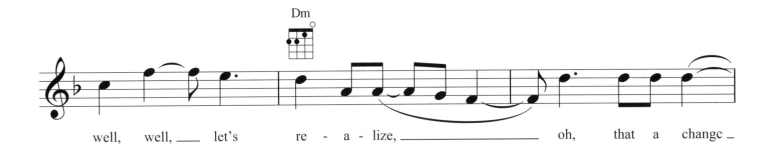

well, well, ___ let's re - a - lize, _____ oh, that a change __

_____ can on - ly come _____ when we _____

stand to-geth-er as one. We are the world, _ _____

Additional Lyrics

2. We can't go on pretending day by day
That someone, somewhere will soon make a change.
We are all a part of God's great big family,
And the truth, you know: love is all we need.

3. Send them your heart so they know that someone cares,
And their lives will be stronger and free.
As God has shown us by turning stone to bread,
And so we all must lend a helping hand.

What the World Needs Now Is Love

Lyric by Hal David
Music by Burt Bacharach

First note

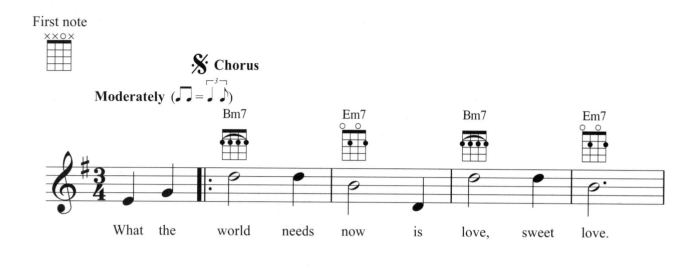

You Light Up My Life

Words and Music by Joseph Brooks

You Raise Me Up

Words and Music by Brendan Graham and Rolf Lovland

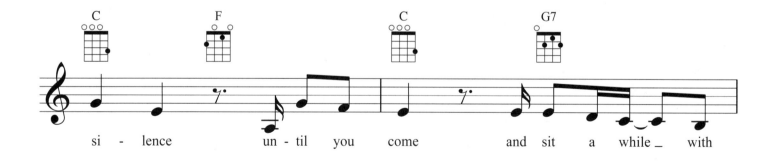

You'll Never Walk Alone

from CAROUSEL
Lyrics by Oscar Hammerstein II
Music by Richard Rodgers

lark. _____ Walk on through the

wind, Walk on through the rain, Tho' your

dreams be tossed and blown. _____ Walk

on, walk on, with hope in your heart, And you'll

nev - er walk a - lone, _____ You'll

nev - er walk a - lone! _____

You've Got a Friend

Words and Music by Carole King

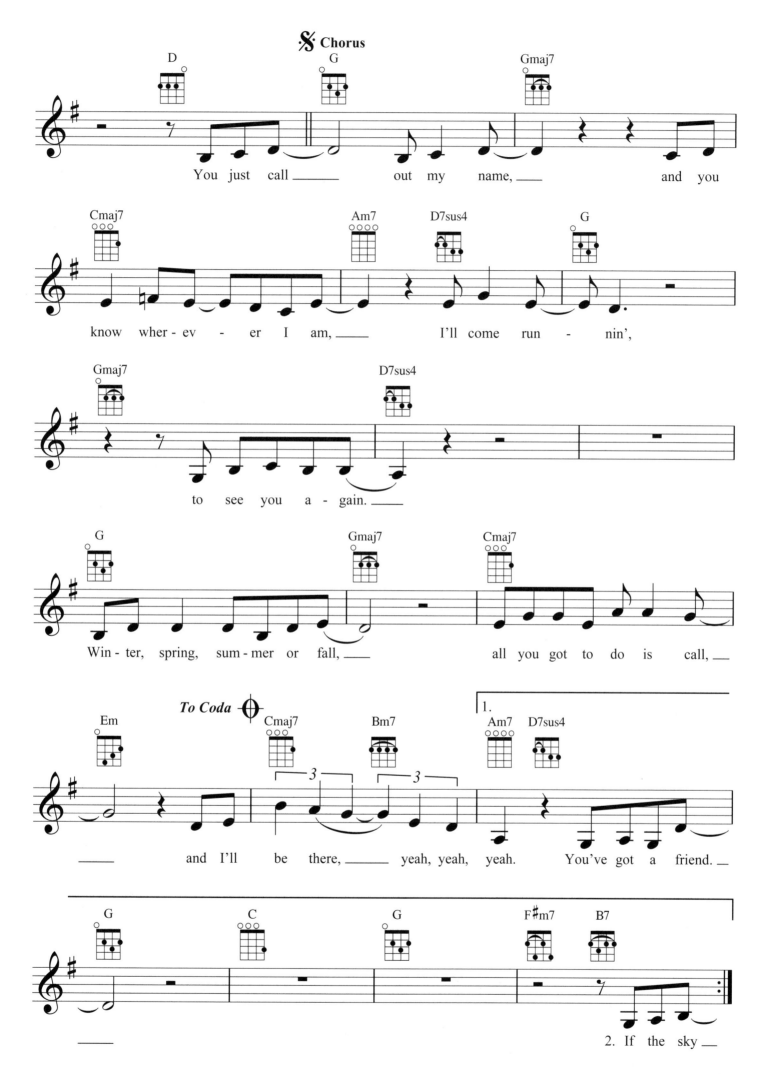

Additional Lyrics

2. If the sky above you should turn dark and full of clouds
   And that old North wind should begin to blow,
   Keep your head together and call my name out loud, now.
   Soon I'll be knockin' upon your door.